DEFENDING THE NATION

Defending the Nation

THE AIR FORCE

John Hamilton
ABDO Publishing Company

visit us at
www.abdopublishing.com

Cover Photos: front, U.S. Air Force; back, U.S. Air Force
Interior Photos: AP Images p. 23; Corbis pp. 1, 4, 5, 9, 14; Peter Arnold p. 21; U.S. Air Force pp. 8, 10-11, 13, 15, 17, 19, 20, 22, 25, 26, 27, 29

Series Coordinator: Megan M. Gunderson
Editors: Rochelle Baltzer, Megan M. Gunderson
Art Direction & Cover Design: Neil Klinepier

Library of Congress Cataloging-in-Publication Data

Hamilton, John.
  The Air Force / John Hamilton.
     p. cm. -- (Defending the nation)
  Includes index.
  ISBN-13: 978-1-59679-753-6
  ISBN-10: 1-59679-753-3
  1. United States. Air Force--History. 2. United States. Air Force--History, Military. I. Title II.
Series: Hamilton, John, 1959- . Defending the nation.

  UG633.H355 2006
  358.400973--dc22

                                                            2005029895

Contents

The U.S. Air Force

The U.S. military is among the most powerful on Earth. It exists to protect America and its people. The military is trained to destroy America's enemies. But it also assists people during natural disasters. When hurricanes or earthquakes strike, the U.S. military is often there to help.

The U.S. Air Force is one branch of the U.S. military. The United States has the most modern air force in the world. The air force can employ missiles to strike an enemy thousands of miles away. It even controls **satellites** in space! The air force uses fighter jets to combat enemies in the air. Its airplanes also support troops on the ground.

More than 3,000 active-duty U.S. Air Force members work for the Air Force Recruiting Service. Posters are one way of attracting new recruits.

Like all the armed forces, it is the air force's job to preserve the peace and security of the United States. The men and women of today's U.S. Air Force are volunteers. They willingly give their time, and sometimes their lives, to defend their country.

Timeline

1860 - The U.S. Army Signal Corps was formed.

1861 - The army used observation balloons during the beginning of the American Civil War.

1903 - On December 17, Orville and Wilbur Wright made the first flight in a heavier-than-air powered aircraft.

1907 - On August 1, the Signal Corps established its Aeronautical Division.

1909 - On August 2, the Signal Corps purchased *Signal Corps Airplane No. 1* from the Wright brothers.

1918 - On May 24, the Air Service of the U.S. Army was created.

1926 - The Air Service was renamed the Air Corps.

1941 - On June 20, the Air Corps and the Air Force Combat Command were combined to form the Army Air Forces.

1947 - On July 26, the U.S. Air Force became an independent branch of the armed forces.

1954 - The Air Force Academy was established in Colorado.

Fun Facts

• Each branch of the U.S. armed forces has an official song. Composer Robert Crawford beat out nearly 800 other entrants in a contest to choose a song for the air force. Now officially titled "The U.S. Air Force," Crawford's song was introduced on September 2, 1939.

• When World War II began, there were fewer than 30,000 U.S. airmen. But during the war, the air force grew rapidly. By 1945, more than 2.2 million men and women were employed by the air force. And, its fleet contained more than 65,000 aircraft.

History of the Air Force

Before the U.S. Air Force existed, military air activities were part of the U.S. Army. The U.S. Army Signal Corps was formed in 1860 to oversee army communications. Beginning in 1861, the army used observation balloons for **reconnaissance** during the American **Civil War**. Balloons were also used during the **Spanish-American War** in 1898.

Orville and Wilbur Wright

Just five years later, Orville and Wilbur Wright changed the future of flight. On December 17, 1903, the Wright brothers flew a heavier-than-air airplane. This historic 12-second powered flight is considered the first of its kind! By 1905, the Wright brothers had built the world's first practical airplane. Gradually, they gained worldwide fame with their invention.

On August 1, 1907, the Signal Corps established its **Aeronautical** Division. After this, the Wright brothers assumed the U.S.

government would be their primary customer. But at first, the government wasn't interested in airplanes.

Then on August 2, 1909, the Signal Corps purchased its first airplane from the Wright brothers. It was called the Wright 1909 Military Flyer. Officially, the army called it *Signal Corps Airplane No. 1.*

Over the next three years, the Signal Corps acquired more aircraft. It also began to train brave pilots to fly these new machines.

Orville piloted the first flight on December 17, 1903. Then, he and Wilbur took turns. On the fourth and longest flight of the day, Wilbur flew 852 feet (260 m) in 59 seconds.

The first U.S. Army unit devoted only to **aviation** was established on March 3, 1913. It was called the First Provisional Aero Squadron. On December 8, it officially became the First Aero Squadron. This squadron was the U.S. Army's first air combat unit. It flew during an expedition along the Mexican border in 1916. However, the mission proved that the U.S. aviation program was not yet ready for combat.

By 1917, the First Aero Squadron was still the only fully-equipped air unit the U.S. Army had. Several European countries had more advanced aviation forces than the United States. So when the United States entered **World War I**, most American combat pilots were trained by the French.

American **aviation** services continued to grow and improve. On May 24, 1918, the Air Service of the U.S. Army was created. The Air Service participated in just nine months of the war. During that time, its nearly 800 aircraft provided **reconnaissance** and battlefield support. The Air Service also downed 756 enemy aircraft.

Following **World War I**, the United States improved the training of its air force. In 1926, the Air Service was renamed the Air Corps. On June 20, 1941, the Air Corps combined with the Air Force Combat Command under one name. Still part of the army, they were now called the Army Air Forces (AAF).

In World War I, airplanes fought each other in aerial duels called dogfights. Both British and American forces used the Sopwith Camel to win battles in the sky.

The AAF fought fierce air battles during **World War II**. And in 1945, America dropped two **atomic bombs** on Japan. Two long-range B-29 aircraft named the *Enola Gay* and the *Bockscar* bombed Hiroshima and Nagasaki. Both cities were destroyed, and thousands of people died. After this, World War II finally ended.

Long-range bombers and **nuclear** weapons meant that the AAF had become powerful and important. So in 1946, the Strategic Air Command (SAC) was formed to oversee the use of these tools.

The U.S. government realized that a separate air division within the military was necessary. On July 26, 1947, the AAF became an independent part of America's armed forces, just like the army or the navy. At this time, the AAF was renamed the U.S. Air Force.

During the second half of the 1900s, the air force focused on new technology and highly trained airmen. These developments made the U.S. Air Force the most powerful in the world.

The air force played substantial roles in both the **Korean War** and the **Vietnam War**. America's air power also was important during conflicts in the Persian Gulf in 1991 and in Kosovo, Yugoslavia, in 1999.

The Bockscar *is on display at the National Museum of the U.S. Air Force at Wright-Patterson Air Force Base in Dayton, Ohio.*

Terrorists attacked the United States on September 11, 2001. That year, the U.S. Air Force led the way during America's invasion of Afghanistan. It also helped the United States invade Iraq in 2003. The air force remains an important part of the continuing fight against terrorism.

Famous U.S. Aviators

Captain Eddie Rickenbacker

Throughout U.S. Air Force history, brave **aviators** have led the way. Captain Edward "Eddie" Rickenbacker was a fighter pilot in **World War I**. By the end of the war, he had shot down 22 airplanes. On November 6, 1930, Rickenbacker earned the Medal of Honor for his efforts. This is the highest award given to U.S. military personnel.

General Henry H. "Hap" Arnold helped make the United States an aerial superpower. Arnold learned to fly from the Wright brothers. He was one of the first military pilots. During **World War II**, he was the commanding general of the AAF. In 1944, Arnold became the first five-star general of the air force. This rank is given only in wartime.

General Charles E. "Chuck" Yeager was a fighter pilot in World War II. He was also a very skilled test pilot. On October 14, 1947, Yeager became the first person to fly faster than the speed of sound. He did this in a rocket-powered Bell X-1 aircraft named *Glamorous Glennis*.

Colonel Jacqueline "Jackie" Cochran helped pave the way for women in **aviation**. During **World War II**, she directed the Women's Air Force Service Pilots (WASP) program. Then in 1953, she became the first woman to break the sound barrier. During her career, Cochran held the most speed, altitude, and distance records of any pilot.

Record-breakers Chuck Yeager and Jackie Cochran were friends for many years.

Organization

The mission of the U.S. Air Force is to defend and protect the United States through air and space power. Pilots are only one part of the air force. Airmen hold many other jobs that contribute to its mission. In 2003, there were about 368,000 active-duty airmen serving in the U.S. Air Force. Women made up about 20 percent of this group.

The U.S. military, including the air force, is organized by a hierarchy. That means there are many levels of authority. The head of the U.S. military is the president of the United States. He or she is called the commander in chief. A four-star general called the chief of staff is the top military leader within the air force.

Below the chief of staff, there are officers and **enlisted** airmen. Officers are specially trained in leadership skills. They make big decisions and have more responsibility than enlisted airmen. Only officers can be pilots. But enlisted airmen can hold supporting jobs aboard aircraft, such as aerial gunners or flight engineers.

Ranks

There are many ranks for U.S. Air Force airmen. A rank is a level of responsibility. Airmen can be promoted to a higher rank for length of service, additional education, and success on the battlefield. Symbols attached to an airman's uniform represent his or her rank.

Officer Ranks

Second Lieutenant (O-1)

First Lieutenant (O-2)

Captain (O-3)

Major (O-4)

Lieutenant Colonel (O-5)

Colonel (O-6)

Brigadier General (O-7)

Major General (O-8)

Lieutenant General (O-9)

General (O-10)

General of the Air Force
(Wartime only)

The letter and number next to each rank indicates a person's pay grade.

Enlisted Ranks

Airman Basic (E-1)

Airman (E-2)

Airman First Class (E-3)

Senior Airman (E-4)

Staff Sergeant (E-5)

Technical Sergeant (E-6)

Master Sergeant (E-7)

First Sergeant (E-7)

Senior Master Sergeant (E-8)

First Sergeant (E-8)

Chief Master Sergeant (E-9)

First Sergeant (E-9)

Command Chief
Master Sergeant (E-9)

Chief Master Sergeant
of the Air Force (E-9)

Training

Persons between the ages of 17 and 27 are able to **enlist** in the U.S. Air Force. Men and women must complete high school before enlisting. Also, they must pass a physical exam. A written test called the Armed Services Vocational Aptitude Battery (ASVAB) helps determine which career an enlistee should pursue.

Enlisted air force candidates, or recruits, begin Basic Military Training (BMT) at Lackland Air Force Base in San Antonio, Texas. BMT is both physically and mentally challenging. In six and a half weeks, recruits become physically fit. They learn how to take orders. And, they undergo weapons and combat training.

After BMT, new airmen report to air force technical training. These programs allow airmen to study a specific career field. They learn job skills such as aircraft maintenance, medical services, and firefighting. After technical training, airmen report for duty at an air base for their first assignment.

The fifth week of Basic Military Training is called "Warrior Week."
Once completed, a recruit has the privilege of being called an airman.

New recruits taking the oath of enlistment

Men and women can apply to become officers if they are between ages 17 and 34. An air force officer needs more education and training than an **enlisted** airman. Officers can become pilots, navigators, or aerospace engineers.

There are several ways to become an air force officer. Some trainees attend the U.S. Air Force Academy in Colorado Springs, Colorado. There, an officer in training is called a cadet.

The Air Force Academy is a highly selective, demanding four-year college. It was established on April 1, 1954. Women first attended in 1976.

If a person has already graduated from college, he or she may attend Basic Officer Training (BOT) at the U.S. Air Force's Officer Training School. This program is located at Maxwell Air Force Base near Montgomery, Alabama. BOT is a 12-week program that teaches leadership skills. Approximately 1,000 officers graduate from the program each year.

Cadets undergo intense training at the U.S. Air Force Academy.

All future airmen take an oath to join the U.S. Air Force. **Enlistees** take the oath of enlistment, while future officers take the oath of office. Although the oaths are different, every future airman promises to "support and defend the Constitution of the United States against all enemies." This is one of the first steps to joining the U.S. Air Force.

There are several other ways to become a member of the U.S. Air Force. Some people join the Air Force Reserve Officers' Training Corps (ROTC). This program exists in more than 1,000 colleges nationwide, as well as in Puerto Rico. Cadets attend regular college courses, while also learning air force history, military procedures, and leadership skills. Upon graduation, they serve at least four years.

Both the Air National Guard and the Air Force Reserve use a variety of aircraft to transport troops and equipment worldwide.

The Air National Guard is another way to become a part of the U.S. Air Force. More than 100,000 men and women serve in the Air National Guard. In times of need, the federal or state government may

The Air National Guard is in every U.S. state and territory, as well as the District of Columbia.

call guard members into service. At home and abroad, they support relief efforts after natural disasters, such as hurricanes.

The Air Force Reserve is similar to the Air National Guard. Reservists are called into active duty when the air force needs additional forces. Reserve airmen are trained to be ready to serve their nation at a moment's notice. To be prepared, they train one weekend a month and two weeks a year. Most reservists also have **civilian** jobs.

In Flight

One of the most important jobs of the U.S. Air Force is **reconnaissance**. The air force has many tools to accomplish this task. These include high-tech electronic systems such as detailed maps, radar tracking, and Global Positioning Systems (GPS). The air force is more successful on the battlefield because of the information it gathers.

The MQ-1 Predator is an airplane with no pilot. Instead, trained people on the ground fly it by remote control. The Predator is 27 feet (8 m) long and has cameras and sensors that collect data. Sometimes, Predators are also armed with powerful missiles.

The air force also uses aircraft to fight enemy airplanes. This is called air-to-air combat. Air-to-air combat jets such as the F-22A Raptor can also strike targets on the ground.

The F-16 Fighting Falcon is a highly useful fighter aircraft. It can travel more than 2,000 miles (3,200 km). And, it can reach speeds of 1,500 miles per hour (2,400 km/hr). The F-16 is also dual-purpose. It can fight other airplanes as well as bomb targets on the ground. And, the F-16 can attack day or night in any kind of weather.

The F-117A Nighthawk is the world's first **stealth** fighter. It is very hard for enemy radar to find the F-117A. This makes the F-117A ideal for sneaking into enemy territory and bombing important targets.

F-16 Fighting Falcon

Long-range bombers are often much larger and slower than fighter jets. But, they can travel long distances at great heights. And, they can carry huge loads of heavy bombs. Some bombers even carry **nuclear** weapons.

The U.S. Air Force has relied on the B-52 Stratofortress since the 1950s. From wingtip to wingtip, the B-52 measures 185 feet (56 m). That is more than half the length of a football field! It can fly for thousands of miles, deep into enemy territory. Once there, it can drop many kinds of bombs and missiles.

The B-1B Lancer is a long-range bomber that can fly faster than the speed of sound. It was first used in 1998 during combat in the Middle East. Today, it continues to help with operations in that region.

The B-2 Spirit is a long-range bomber that uses **stealth** technology. It has specially coated,

The B-1B Lancer has broken speed records.

swept wings that make it look like a bat. It is very difficult for an enemy to spot. The B-2 can carry many kinds of bombs and missiles, including **nuclear** weapons. This dangerous aircraft is expensive. Each airplane costs more than $1 billion to produce!

A B-52 Stratofortress can be refueled in midair! This increases the amount of time and the distance it can travel.

The Future of the Force

The U.S. Air Force of the future will rely on advanced technology. Skilled airmen and ground support crews will quickly complete missions anywhere in the world.

Some futuristic technology is already a reality for the air force. An increasingly important part of the air force is Air Force Space Command. It uses **satellites** for many purposes, including learning about enemy forces. With the information it gathers, Air Force Space Command helps protect national security.

The air force will continue learning to respond quickly and forcefully to future threats. This ensures that it will use the best-trained fighters and the most advanced technology available. In this way, the U.S. Air Force will be ready for whatever the future holds.

The U.S. Air Force does more than just continue improving war-related technology. The air force also continues its mission of humanitarian aid. This includes helping victims of the 2004 Asian tsunami (right) and Hurricane Katrina in 2005.

Glossary

aeronautics - a science dealing with the design, manufacture, and operation of aircraft.

atomic bomb - a bomb that uses the energy of atoms. It is thousands of times more powerful than a regular bomb.

aviation - the operation and navigation of aircraft. A person that operates an aircraft is called an aviator.

civil war - a war between groups in the same country. The United States of America and the Confederate States of America fought a civil war from 1861 to 1865.

civilian - of or relating to something nonmilitary.

enlist - to join the armed forces voluntarily. An enlistee is a person who enlists for military service.

Korean War - from 1950 to 1953. A war between North and South Korea. The U.S. government sent troops to help South Korea.

nuclear - of or relating to the energy created when atoms are divided or combined. An atomic bomb is a nuclear weapon.

reconnaissance (rih-KAH-nuh-zuhnts) - an inspection the military uses to gain information about enemy territory.

satellite - a manufactured object that orbits Earth.

Spanish-American War - a war between the United States and Spain in 1898. At the end of the war, Spain freed Cuba and signed over Guam, the Philippines, and Puerto Rico to the United States.

stealth - an action or a behavior performed in a secretive or sneaky manner.

terrorism - the use of terror, violence, or threats to frighten people into action. A person who commits an act of terrorism is called a terrorist.

Vietnam War - from 1957 to 1975. A long, failed attempt by the United States to stop North Vietnam from taking over South Vietnam.

World War I - from 1914 to 1918, fought in Europe. Great Britain, France, Russia, the United States, and their allies were on one side. Germany, Austria-Hungary, and their allies were on the other side.

World War II - from 1939 to 1945, fought in Europe, Asia, and Africa. Great Britain, France, the United States, the Soviet Union, and their allies were on one side. Germany, Italy, Japan, and their allies were on the other side.

Web Sites

To learn more about the U.S. Air Force, visit ABDO Publishing Company on the World Wide Web at **www.abdopublishing.com**. Web sites about the U.S. Air Force are featured on our Book Links page. These links are routinely monitored and updated to provide the most current information available.

Index